WALCH WORKPLACE SKILLS SERIES

Problems in
Manufacturing

WILLIAM WEBB SPRAGUE

J. Weston Walch, Publisher

Portland, Maine

1 2 3 4 5 6 7 8 9 10

ISBN 0-8251-2468-9

DEDICATION

To my parents

Contents

Acknowledgments

Barber Foods

National Semiconductor Corporation

Irwin Tool

To the Learner

The world of <u>manufacturing</u> offers some of the best jobs in the <u>global economy</u>. In this book, you will learn some of the skills manufacturing workers need.

You should know how to add, subtract, multiply, and divide and work with fractions, decimals, and percent. You should be comfortable with common calculators and know how to make estimates.

You will be asked to <u>master</u> basic measurement skills and learn how to read simple drawings, <u>scales</u>, and <u>graphs</u>. You will also learn how to <u>substitute</u> letters for numbers when finding the <u>dimensions</u> of rectangles and squares.

You will work with some examples of the <u>metric system</u>, in keeping with recent changes in manufacturing.

This book will provide you with the basic skills you need in order to learn how to use modern machinery and processes. You may work at operating and maintaining <u>computer numerical control</u>, <u>flexible manufacturing</u>, <u>work cells</u>, and other computer-based machinery.

This book uses examples taken from real manufacturing jobs, with people in a factory working as a team, using their workplace skills to produce quality products.

You will continue to work with communication and reasoning skills. Unfamiliar words and terms used in the manufacturing workplace are underlined and defined at the end of this book.

Like problems in the workplace, many of the problems in this book do not have right or wrong answers. Your job is to find as good an answer as possible.

Chapter 1

Understanding the Job

In this book, you will work with Kim. An experienced worker, Kim was just <u>promoted</u> to a new job.

Kim is a native English speaker and high school graduate. He was not promoted until now because his reading, writing, and math skills were not strong enough for him to understand the new <u>technology</u> coming <u>on-line</u> at the company.

Kim has enrolled in an adult education program to work on his reading, writing, and math skills. His company supports his interest in learning and helps him attend this program.

■ **SHARP - Skills Development and Enhancement Program**

■ **Basic and Intermediate Core Courses**

- ● **E.S.L. (English as a Second Language)**
- ● **Basic and Intermediate Workplace Communications (Reading Comprehension/Writing/Vax Literacy**
- ● **Basic and General Mathematics (Math 1 + 2)**
- ● **Technical Mathematics (Math 3) Parts 1 + 2**

■ **Advanced Courses**

- ●
- ●
- ●
- ●
- ●

This part of the Skills Development Program is in the planning stage:

We would sincerely appreciate any and all comments or suggestions from you— our customers!

An outline for a company workplace skills program.
Courtesy of National Semiconductor Corporation.

First see how Kim's new job fits in with other jobs in his company. Then think of ways he can help improve the work of the team.

Congratulations

After 10 years with the Armond Tool Company, Kim has been promoted to <u>second shift</u> shipping/receiving <u>supervisor</u>. Before this promotion, Kim was a machine operator on the first shift.

Kim does not know anyone on the second shift. He was given this job for two reasons: 1. His experience. 2. His ability to get along with different kinds of people.

Kim supervises two people, Lida and Chirk. Lida is a machine repair worker from the former Soviet Union. She has been in the United States for only three years. Chirk, recently arrived from Cambodia, has just started working with the new <u>data entry system</u>.

From time to time, Kim will work with about 10 other people. Half of them have recently come to the United States from other countries. He is not their boss, but he is responsible for their work.

Kim's boss is Janet, the shipping/receiving manager. She works on the first shift. Kim rarely speaks with Janet because they are on different shifts. Usually Kim must report to her in writing.

Kim must report problems on his shift to Theodore, the second shift manager. Plans must be talked over with Janet. Every week Kim has a meeting with Janet and other managers.

A New Assignment

In his new job, Kim must first learn about the work of the people on the second shift <u>loading dock</u>. Then he can find ways to help them improve production and work quality.

In fact, this is Kim's first special assignment in his new job. He must recommend ways to improve worker performance on the second shift loading dock. He has to give his report to Janet in her office next month.

Kim can recommend ways to organize work on his shift. Management has to approve any changes. Kim cannot hire new workers.

READING PEOPLE MAPS:

Kim's first task is to find out how his new job fits in with other jobs at the company. One way to do this is to read an <u>organizational chart</u> (next page). This drawing is like a map of company people.

Like most maps, organizational charts make things smaller than they really are. This is done on an organizational chart by using <u>abbreviations</u> of words. Then the words can fit in the boxes on the chart.

Abbreviations are like your <u>initials</u>. For example, Kim's full name is Kim Pham, but people in the workplace call him K.P., which is short for his full name—Kim Pham.

PROBLEM 1:

To make his plan, Kim needs to find the meaning of the abbreviations on the chart.

Step 1: Review the chart on the next page to find out if you know what all the abbreviations mean. For example, the abbreviation MGR. means manager, SHP./RECEIVNG means Shipping and Receiving, and QC/QA means <u>Quality Control/Quality Assurance</u>.

Step 2: Write the full word for each of the abbreviations used. For example, ACCT. stands for accountant.

a. ACCT.   *accountant*   h. MECH.   _____

b. ADMIN.   _____   i. 2ND   _____

c. &   _____   j. SFT.   _____

d. 1ST   _____   k. S/R   _____

e. MAINT.   _____   l. SUPER.   _____

f. MGR./ACCT. _____   m. V.P.   _____

g. MKT.   _____

A period (.) usually goes at the end of an abbreviation.

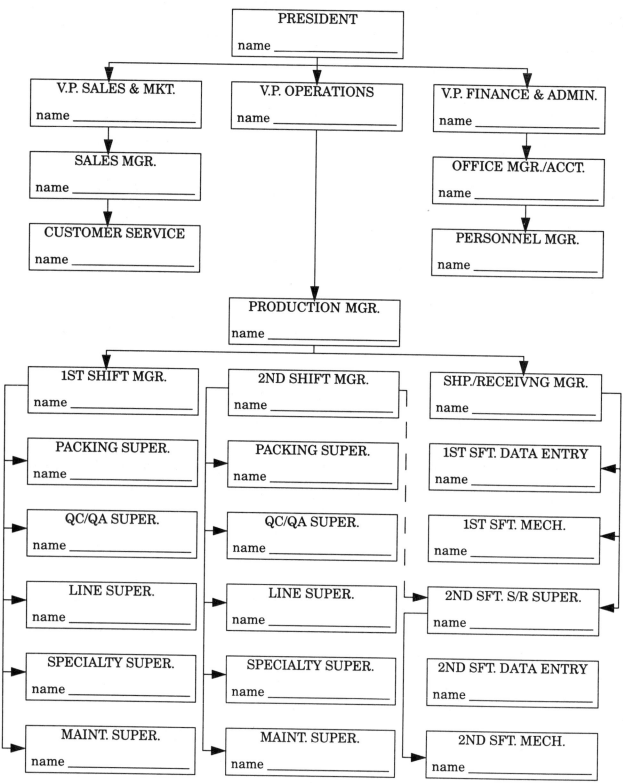

ARMOND TOOL ORGANIZATIONAL CHART:
Managers and Supervisors

QUESTION:

Abbreviations often differ from company to company. Give two meanings for the abbreviation "Super":

1.

2.

PROBLEM 2:

Kim needs to put the names of the people he works with in their separate boxes on the organizational chart.

Step 1: Review "Congratulations" (page 2).

Step 2: Put the names of Kim, Lida, Chirk, Janet, and Theodore where they belong on the chart.

QUESTIONS AND ACTIVITIES:

1. Why is there a solid line between Kim and Janet?

2. Why is there a dotted line between Kim and Theodore?

3. Do you see any problems in finding out who's "really" the boss?

4. Not all organizational charts are exactly the same, because not all organizations are exactly the same. If you can, put the names of some of the people in your workplace in the boxes with no names on this organizational chart.

5. Ask your boss or someone in your company's <u>Personnel Department</u> to show you an organizational chart of your workplace.

6. Make an organizational chart of the people in your workplace. Don't forget to put your name and your job in it.

Writing an Overview

Kim now knows where his new job fits in with other jobs. He will use this information in his final report, recommending ways to improve worker performance on the second shift loading dock.

The first part of Kim's report will be a topic sentence, which will be an <u>overview</u> of his report. To make the overview, Kim will need to know Who, What, Where, When, and Why.

PROBLEM 3:

Help Kim find Who, What, Where, When, and Why about his report.

Step 1: Review "Congratulations" and "A New Assignment" (page 4).

Step 2: Review the organizational chart for Armond Tool Company (page 4).

Step 3: Now write down your answers to Who, Where, and When about Kim's plan. What and Why are answered for you.

Who?

What? Kim's plan for improvement

Where?

When?

Why? To improve worker performance on the second shift loading dock

PROBLEM 4:

Tell in your own words what Kim's plan involves. Tell this in an overview. An overview is like a topic sentence.

The overview should be based on your notes about Kim's plan. It should include the answers to Who, What, Where, When, and Why from Problem 3. Add words to the sentence to help it make sense. This will be the first sentence in your report.

Report Overview (Topic Sentence)

Chapter 2

Making People Points and Number Pictures

In this unit, Kim will find the facts he needs to know before he can finish his report. He must take notes on people and make maps with numbers.

Taking Notes

When you wrote the overview, you put Kim's assignment in your own words. Now you will have to find facts. These short-answer questions will help you find the facts about Kim's workplace team.

First, review the introduction, "Congratulations," "A New Assignment," and the organizational chart from Chapter 1 (page 4).

Now, write your answers to the following questions:

QUESTIONS:

1. Name two strengths that Kim brings to his new job as second shift shipping/receiving supervisor.

   a.

   b.

2. What are Kim's weaknesses in basic skills?

   a.

   b.

   c.

3. What is Kim doing to strengthen these skills?

4. Why is it important for Kim to strengthen these skills?

5. What skills do these people offer the company?

   Lida:

   Chirk:

6. Describe one way Lida and Chirk are like each other.

7. Name one problem Lida and Chirk could bring to work at the loading dock.

Number Maps

In "A New Assignment," you found that some problems exist in shipping and receiving. Management now says that in 1994, second shift production will be down 10% from the high of 1993. In 1993 the company shipped 10,000 packages of product from the second shift.

Management also found an increase in the number of packages shipped to the wrong customers from the second shift. In 1993 1% of the shipments were sent to wrong customers. Next year the number of wrong shipments will increase to 2%.

Kim has one month to write a plan to deal with these problems. His goals are:

1. In 1994, to stop the decrease in production.

2. In 1994, to stop the increase in mistakes.

3. In 1996, to show a 10% increase over 1993 in production.

4. In 1996, to decrease the number of packages shipped to the wrong customers to 1%.

Reading the organizational chart helped Kim find how people in his company work together. He also found the strengths and weaknesses that people brought to their jobs.

These facts will help Kim set goals. These goals will help him make a plan to improve the production and the quality of the work on second shift shipping and receiving.

Making Graphs

Kim must show management in numbers what he plans to do. Kim must show by year:

1. When the decrease in production will stop.

2. When the increase in mistakes will stop.

3. When production will reach 10% over 1993.

4. When quality will reach 1% of number of packages shipped to the wrong customers.

Like words, numbers must be written down in a way that other people can understand. Kim will now organize his plans in numbers so that other people can understand his goals. He will make graphs to help explain his plan.

An organizational chart is a map of persons. A <u>graph</u> is a map of numbers. Graphs show a picture of how numbers work together. One side of the graph shows one thing, and the bottom of the graph shows something else. The picture they make is based on how these two sides work together.

Bar Graphs

When the number picture on a graph shows in the form of bars (stripes or bands), the graph is called a <u>bar graph</u>. Kim decides to show some of the facts about shipping by using bar graphs.

PROBLEM 1:

Kim needs to complete a chart of the numbers for his plan about shipping.

PROCEDURE:

Complete the following chart of percentages and whole numbers. Try to estimate the missing answers without using a calculator. Fill in the missing answers.

Year	Number of Packages Shipped	Percentage Increase/Decrease
1993	10,000	0%
1994	9,000	−10% from 1993
1995	_____	0% from 1994
1996	_____	+10% over 1993

PROBLEM 2:

Help Kim make a graph of the total number of packages shipped by year.

PROCEDURE:

Take the numbers from Problem 1 to make bars on the graph on page 12. Draw each bar up from the year to the line that shows the number of packages shipped that year. Two bars on the graph have been finished as an example. The other bars will look like these two but may be higher or lower or the same.

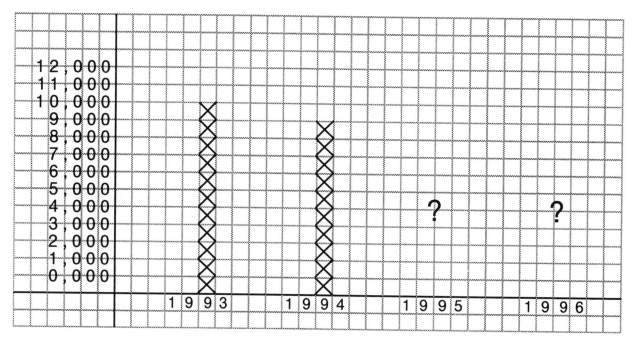

Year and Number of Packages Shipped

PROBLEM 3:

Complete the following chart of percentages and whole numbers. Try to estimate the missing answers without using a calculator. Look back to Problem 1 for the year and number of packages shipped.

PROCEDURE:

Fill in the missing answers.

Year	Number of Wrong Shipments	Percentage of Wrong Shipments
1993	_____	1%
1994	180	2%
1995	_____	2%
1996	110	1%

PROBLEM 4:

Make a graph of the total number of wrong shipments by year.

PROCEDURE:

Take the numbers from Problem 3 to make bars on the graph below. Two bars on the graph have been finished. The other bars will look like these two but may be higher, lower, or the same.

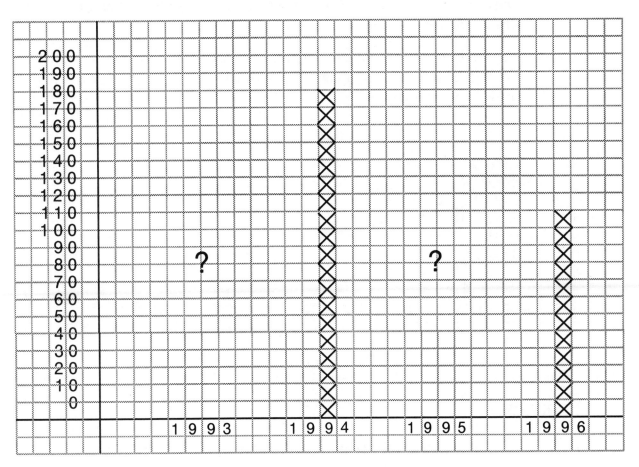

Year and Number of Wrong Shipments

Line Graphs

When the picture on a graph shows in the form of a line, the graph is called a <u>line graph</u>. Kim decides to show some of the facts about shipping by using line graphs.

PROBLEM 5:

Show the figures from Kim's bar graph (page 12) as a line graph.

Step 1: In the graph below, make a dot above each year, on the line that shows the number of packages shipped that year. Two dots are drawn for you.

Step 2: Draw a line connecting the dots on the graph. The line is started for you. Finish it by connecting it with the other two dots you drew in Step 1 above.

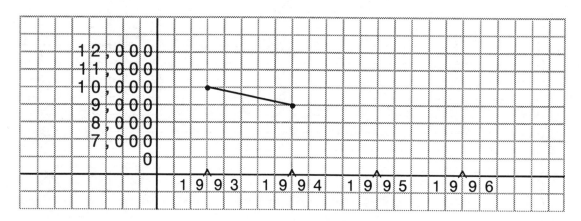

Year and Number of Packages Shipped

PROBLEM 6:

Show the figures from Kim's bar graph (page 13) as a line graph. Your line graph (page 15) will show a picture of the year and number of wrong shipments. Follow Steps 1 and 2 above to make the graph: First draw the dots showing the number of wrong packages shipped each year. Then connect the dots with a line. Two of the dots are drawn for you.

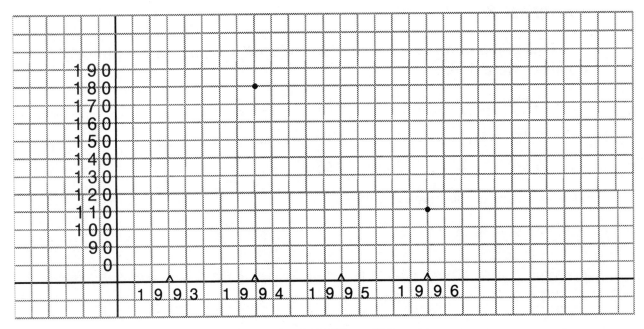

Year and Number of Wrong Shipments

PROBLEM 7:

Make the graph below show the results of first shift shipping. In 1990 the first shift shipped 11,543 packages; in 1991, 10,891; in 1992, 8,755; in 1993, 10,045; in 1994, 8,980; in 1995, 10,450. When making the graph, first round the numbers to the nearest 1,000. The first dot is made for you.

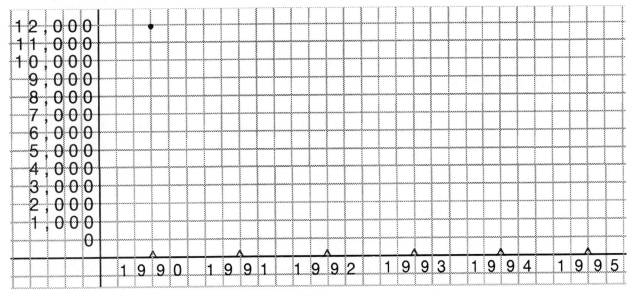

First Shift Shipping

PROBLEM 8:

This graph shows the results of second shift shipping. How many packages were shipped in

1990 _____ ?   1993 _____ ?

1991 _____ ?   1994 _____ ?

1992 _____ ?   1995 _____ ?

Give answers to the nearest 1,000.

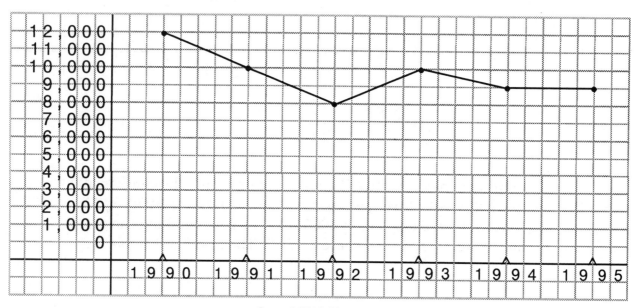

Second Shift Shipping

PROBLEM 9:

This graph (page 17) shows the results of third shift shipping. How many packages were shipped in

1990 _____ ?   1993 _____ ?

1991 _____ ?   1994 _____ ?

1992 _____ ?   1995 _____ ?

Give answers to the nearest 1,000.

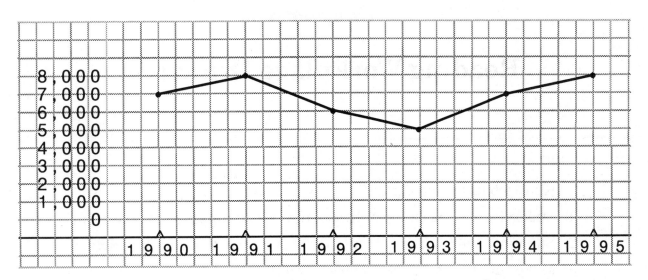

Third Shift Shipping

PROBLEM 10:

Show below that in 1990, Armond Tool shipped 31,000 packages a year; in 1991, 29,000; in 1992, 23,000; in 1993, 25,000; in 1994, 25,000; and in 1995, 27,000.

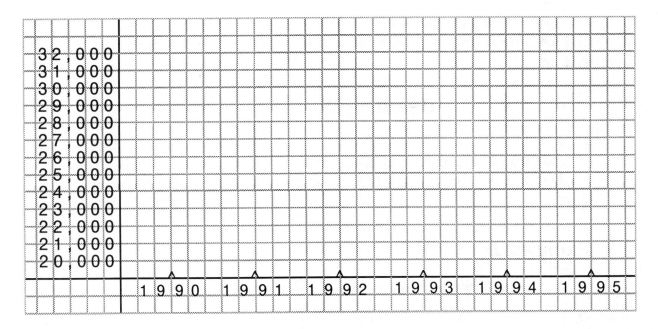

Yearly Shipping

Chapter 3

Reading Workplace Drawings

Kim's job has three parts:

1. Supervise the unloading of trucks that bring supplies into the plant.
2. Supervise the loading of trucks that take away the finished product.
3. Make sure that all workers have supplies where and when they need them.

To do his job, Kim needs to know how the different parts of his workplace work together. One way to understand how things work is to make a drawing. This drawing of his workplace looks like a map of shapes.

Kim's Workplace

The drawing on page 19 is in <u>U.S. customary units</u>, which use inches and feet. Many countries outside the United States use the <u>metric system</u>.

Reading Place Maps

To make his plan, Kim needs to know about his workplace. He also needs to know where Lida and Chirk will be working during the second shift.

PROBLEM 1:

Trace Kim's work. Use the drawing on the next page.

Step 1: Draw a line out of the Loading Dock to Storage I. Draw a line out of the Loading Dock to Storage II.

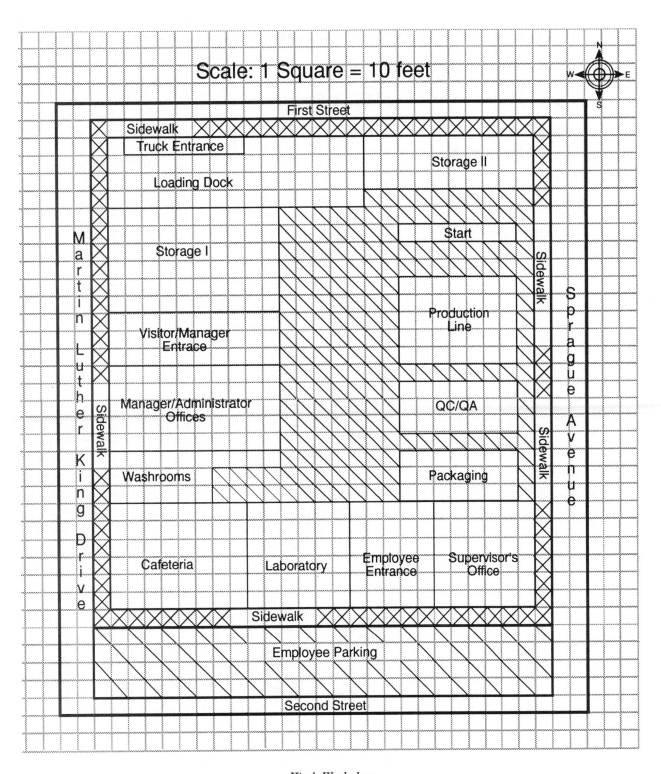

Scale: 1 Square = 10 feet

First Street

Sidewalk

Truck Entrance

Loading Dock

Storage II

Storage I

Start

Martin Luther King Drive

Sidewalk

Visitor/Manager Entrace

Production Line

Manager/Administrator Offices

QC/QA

Washrooms

Packaging

Sidewalk

Sprague Avenue

Cafeteria

Laboratory

Employee Entrance

Supervisor's Office

Sidewalk

Employee Parking

Second Street

Kim's Workplace

Step 2: Draw a line from Storage I to Start; from Storage II to Start.

Step 3: Draw a line from Start to QC/QA.

Step 4: Draw a line from QC/QA to Packaging.

Step 5: Draw a line from Packaging to Storage I; from Packaging to Storage II.

QUESTIONS:

1. Tell one way your job is like Kim's.

2. Tell two ways to make Kim's job easier.

    a.

    b.

Chapter 4

Sizing Up the Workplace

In this unit, you will learn the basics of <u>scales</u> and <u>dimensions</u>. The scales and dimensions of a workplace drawing will give Kim the distance between different places in and near his workplace.

Understanding Scales

Kim's workplace is too big to draw as it is, so on the map it has been made smaller than it really is. Making pictures that are larger or smaller than the way things really are is called drawing to <u>scale</u>. See the drawing on page 22.

For example, you would draw to scale if you wanted to make a map of your town. There is no way to draw a full-size picture of your town on a small piece of paper. So you draw a map to scale. The map scale might be one inch on the map equals one mile in real distance.

The map of Kim's workplace is also drawn to scale. One <u>square</u> on the draft paper equals 10 feet in the workplace.

Reading and Using
Scales and Dimensions

The scale on a map uses one distance to show another distance. You can use scale to find a full answer when you know only part of the answer. For example, the map of Kim's workplace on the next page tells you that one square equals 10 feet. With this information, you can also find that two squares equal 20 feet.

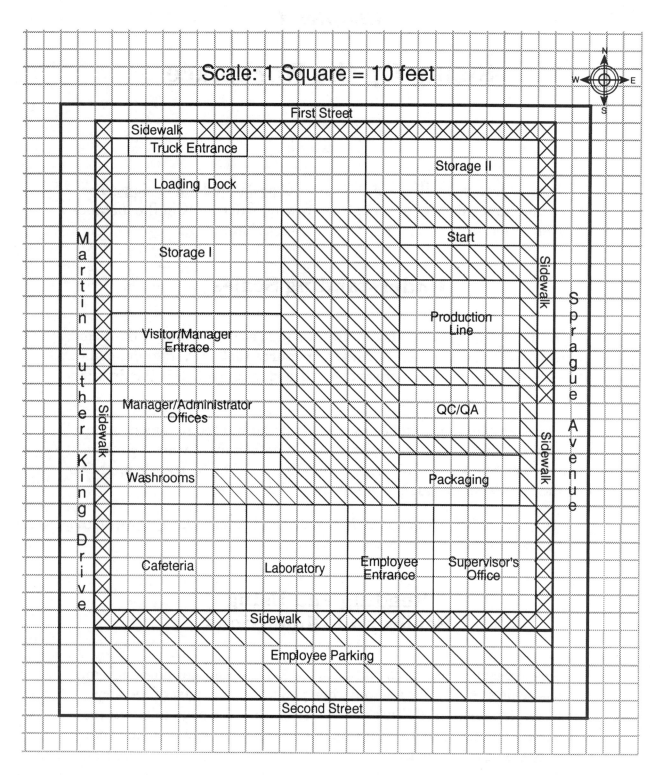

Kim's Workplace and Scale

EXAMPLE 1:

Use the map of Kim's workplace (page 22). Find the distance in yards between the east side of Martin Luther King Drive and the west side of Sprague Avenue.

You know the following information.

1. There are 3 feet in a yard.
2. The map scale reads 1 square equals 10 feet.
3. There are 27 squares between the east side of Martin Luther King Drive and the west side of Sprague Avenue.

Step 1: Multiply 27 (the number of squares) by 10 (the number of feet in each square): 27 x 10 = 270.

The distance you are figuring is 270 feet.

Step 2: Divide 270 (the total number of feet) by 3 (the number of feet in a yard): 270 ÷ 3 = 90

This gives you the number of yards in 270 feet.

Answer: There are 90 yards between the east side of Martin Luther King Drive and the west side of Sprague Avenue.

PROBLEM 1:

Armond Tool wants to change from the U.S. customary system to the metric system. Armond wants to find the approximate distance in <u>meters</u> from the north wall of the building to the south wall.

You know the following information.

1. There are about 3 feet in a meter.
2. The map scale reads 1 square equals 10 feet.
3. There are 28 squares from the north wall of the building to the south wall.

Step 1: Multiply 28 (the number of squares) by 10 (the number of feet in each square): 28 x 10 = _____ feet.

Step 2: Divide _____ (the total number of feet) by 3 (the approximate number of feet in a meter): _____ ÷ 3 = _____ . Round to the nearest whole number.

Answer: There are _____ meters from the north wall of the building to the south wall.

QUESTION:

One meter is approximately three feet. Therefore, one foot equals _____ of a meter. Use either a fraction or a decimal for your answer.

EXAMPLE 2:

Kim wants to use a calculator to find approximately how far Armond Tool is located from the center of Needham, the closest town. He needs the answer in miles. He finds that:

1. His map has two scales. The first scale reads 1 inch equals 1 mile. The second scale reads 1 inch equals 1.6 <u>kilometers</u>.

2. The map shows a distance of about 6.5 inches from Armond Tool to the center of town.

PROCEDURE:

Enter: C	to clear the calculator
Enter: 6.5	(the distance in inches on the map)
Enter: ×	(the sign that means multiply)
Enter: 1	(the number of miles in one inch)
Enter: = or ×	to get the answer

Answer: 6.5 miles

PROBLEM 2:

Find the approximate distance from Armond Tool to the center of Needham. Find the answer in kilometers.

PROCEDURE:

Enter: C	to clear the calculator
Enter: 6.5	(the distance in inches on the map)
Enter: x	(the sign that means multiply)
Enter: 1.6	(the number of kilometers in one inch)
Enter: = or x	to get the answer: _____

Answer: It is _____ kilometers from Armond Tool to the center of Needham.

PROBLEM 3:

Since Kim knows that it is 43 miles from Armond Tool to the center of Hudson, he can <u>convert</u> miles to find kilometers: 1.6 kilometers = 1 mile.

PROCEDURE:

Enter: C	to clear the calculator
Enter: 43	(the number of miles)
Enter: x	(the sign that means multiply)
Enter: 1.6	(the number of kilometers in a mile)
Enter: = or x	to get the answer: _____

Answer: It is _____ kilometers from Armond Tool to the center of Hudson.

PROBLEM 4:

Since Kim knows that it is 57 kilometers from Armond Tool to the center of Camden, he can convert kilometers to find miles: 1 kilometer = .625 miles.

PROCEDURE:

Enter: C	to clear the calculator
Enter: 57	(the number of kilometers)
Enter: x	(the sign that means multiply)
Enter: .625	(the number of miles in a kilometer)
Enter: = or x	to get the answer: _____

Answer: It is _____ miles from Armond Tool to the center of Camden. (Round to the nearest tenth.)

Finding Distances

UPDATE: Management has just told Kim to suggest ways to reorganize the Loading Dock, Storage I, and Storage II.

To do this job, Kim must use the workplace map (page 22). He must find:

1. The distance from the Loading Dock to the Laboratory.
2. The distance from Storage II to the Employee Entrance.
3. The distance from Storage I to the Production Line.
4. The approximate dimensions (the <u>perimeter</u>) of his workplace.
5. The total outside dimensions (the perimeter) formed by the streets around his workplace.
6. The dimensions of Storage I and Storage II and the differences in their perimeters.

Kim knows that as a rule a straight line is the shortest distance between two points. From experience, he knows that the <u>work flow</u> does not always follow this rule.

Kim must first measure the distance between different places in his workplace. If he knows these distances, then he can plan for changes in the placement of Storage I and Storage II.

EXAMPLE 3:

Find the shortest distance from the Loading Dock to the Laboratory.

Step 1: Count the squares from the south side of the Loading Dock to the north side of the Laboratory.

> ***Answer:*** There are 17 squares from the south side of the Loading Dock to the north side of the Laboratory.

Step 2: Multiply 17 × 10 (the number of feet per square).

> ***Answer:*** It is 170 feet from the south side of the Loading Dock to the north side of the Laboratory.

PROBLEM 5:

Find the shortest distance from Storage II to the Employee Entrance. Estimate the missing answers without using a calculator. Fill in the missing answers.

Step 1: Count the squares from the south side of Storage II to the north side of the Employee Entrance: _____

Step 2: Multiply _____ (from Step 1) x 10 (the number of feet per square).

       Answer: It is _____ feet from the south side of Storage II to the north side of the Employee Entrance.

PROBLEM 6:

Find the shortest distance from Storage I to the Production Line. Estimate the missing answers without using a calculator. Fill in the missing answers.

Step 1: Count the squares from the east side of Storage I to the west side of the Production Line: _____

Step 2: Multiply _____ (from Step 1) x _____ (the number of feet per square).

       Answer: It is _____ feet from the east side of Storage I to the west side of the Production Line.

PROBLEM 7:

Find the shortest distance from the south side of Start to the north side of the Production Line. Estimate the missing answers without using a calculator. Fill in the missing answers.

Step 1: Number of squares = _____

Step 2: Multiply the number of squares _____ x _____ (the number of feet per square).

       Answer: _____ feet

Math Practice I

Scales are usually made to show <u>relationships</u>. For example, the map of Kim's workplace used a scale of one square equals one foot. Your town map might have a scale of one inch to one mile. A road map might have a scale of one inch to one hundred miles.

PROBLEM 8:

What lengths do these lines show?

a. Scale: 1 square = 1 inch

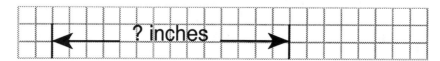

Answer: _____ inches

b. Scale: 1 square = 100 miles

Answer: _____ miles

c. Scale: 1 square = 5 feet

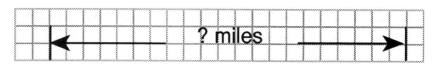

Answer: _____ feet

PROBLEM 9:

Draw a line to scale.

a. Show 11 feet. Scale: 1 square = 1 foot

feet

b. Show 400 miles. Scale: 1 square = 100 miles

miles

c. Show 25 feet. Scale: 1 square = 5 feet

feet

Chapter 5

Around the Workplace

In this unit, you will be asked to work with perimeters. A <u>perimeter</u> is the combined dimensions of all sides of a shape.

Kim's Walk

Kim often walks around his workplace during break. The approximate distance of his walk is between the <u>length</u> of the outside perimeter of his building and the length of the outside perimeter of the sidewalk.

To find the perimeter of a shape, add all its outside dimensions together.

EXAMPLE 1:

Find the outside dimension (the perimeter) of Kim's building. (See the drawing on page 31).

Step 1: Find the length of the north side of the building.

    a. Count the number of squares on the north side of the building: 25.

    b. Multiply 25 x 10 (feet per square).

    Answer: 250 feet

Step 2: Find the length of the west side of the building.

    a. Count the number of squares on the west side of the building: 27.

    b. Multiply 27 x 10 (feet per square).
    Answer: 270 feet

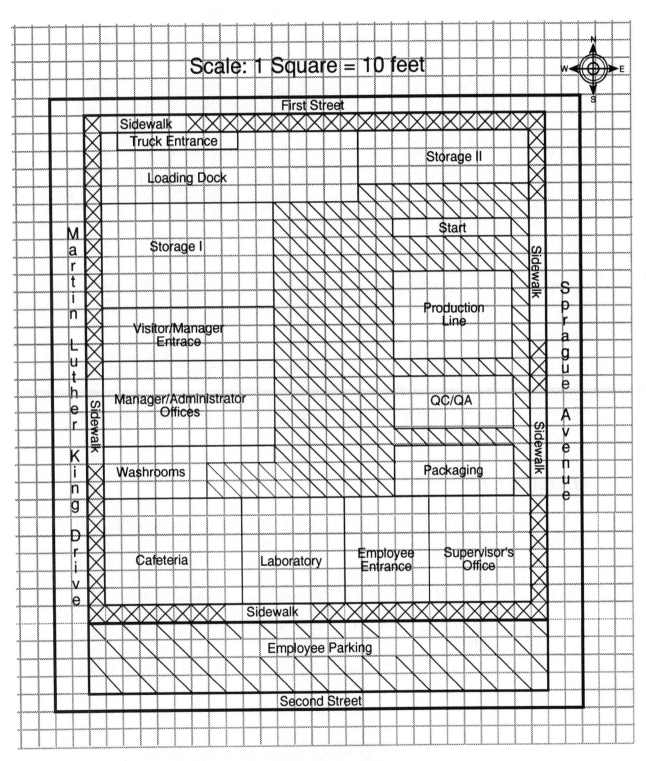

Kim's Workplace Walk

Step 3:   Find the length of the south side of the building.

   a.   Count the number of squares on the south side of the building: 25.

   b.   Multiply 25 x 10 (feet per square).

   Answer: 250 feet

Step 4:   Find the length of the east side of the building.

   a.   Count the number of squares on the east side of the building: 27.

   b.   Multiply 27 x 10 (feet per square).

   Answer: 270 feet

Step 5:   Find the perimeter (the combined dimensions) of the building.

   a.   North side   =   250 feet

   b.   West side   =   +270 feet

   c.   South side   =   +250 feet

   d.   East side   =   +270 feet

   Answer: All sides = 1,040 feet = the perimeter of the building.

PROBLEM 1:

Find the outside dimension (the perimeter) of the sidewalk. Estimate the missing answers without using a calculator. Fill in the missing answers.

Step 1:   Find the outside length of the north side of the sidewalk.

   a.   Count the number of squares on the north side of the sidewalk: _____

   b.   Multiply _____ (the number of north side squares) x 10 (feet per square).

   Answer: _____ feet

Step 2:   Find the outside length of the west side of the sidewalk.

   a.   Count the number of squares on the west side of the sidewalk:

   _____

b. Multiply _____ (the number of west side squares) x 10 (feet per square).

Answer: _____ feet

Step 3: Find the outside length of the south side of the sidewalk.

    a. Count the number of squares on the south side of the sidewalk: _____

    b. Multiply _____ (the number of south side squares) x 10 (feet per square).

    Answer: _____ feet

Step 4: Find the outside length of the east side of the sidewalk.

    a. Count the number of squares on the east side of the sidewalk:

    _____

    b. Multiply _____ (the number of east side squares) x 10 (feet per square).

    Answer: _____ feet

Step 5: Find the total outside dimensions (perimeter) of the sidewalk. Fill in the blanks with your answers to steps 1, 2, 3, and 4.

    a. North side   =   _____ feet

    b. West side   =   +_____ feet

    c. South side   =   +_____ feet

    d. East side   =   +_____ feet

    The perimeter =   1,120 feet

    Answer: Your answer should be: All sides = 1,120 feet = the perimeter of the sidewalk.

How far does Kim walk? Since he walks on the sidewalk, Kim walks a distance between the outside perimeter of the sidewalk, which is 1,120 feet, and the outside perimeter of the building, which is 1,040 feet. Kim walks between 1,120 and 1,040 feet.

Neighborhood Perimeters

The streets around Kim's workplace form another perimeter. Kim's workplace is built on a lot bounded by Martin Luther King Drive, First Street, Sprague Avenue, and Second Street. Trucks enter and leave the Loading Dock from First Street. The Employee Entrance is on Second Street, and the Visitor/Manager Entrance is on Martin Luther King Drive. Employee Parking is entered from Second Street.

PROBLEM 2:

Find the outside perimeter of the shape made by the <u>intersections</u> of Martin Luther King Drive, First Street, Sprague Avenue, and Second Street. Estimate the missing answers without using a calculator. Fill in the missing answers.

Step 1: There are 35 squares from the north side of First Street to the south side of Second Street along Martin Luther King Drive. Multiply 35 × 10 (feet per square).

Answer: 350 feet

Step 2: There are 31 squares from the west side of Martin Luther King Drive to the east side of Sprague Avenue along First Street. Multiply 31 × 10 (feet per square).

Answer: 310 feet

Step 3: Find the number of squares from the north side of First Street to the south side of Second Street along Sprague Avenue. Multiply

_____ (the number of squares) × 10 (feet per square).

Answer: _____ feet

Step 4: Find the number of squares from the west side of Martin Luther King Drive to the east side of Sprague Avenue along Second Street. Multiply _____ (the number of squares) × 10 (feet per square).

Answer: _____ feet

Step 5: Find the total outside perimeter of the shape made by the intersections of Martin Luther King Drive, First Street, Sprague Avenue, and Second Street.

    a. = 350 feet   (the distance from the north side of First Street to the south side of Second Street along Martin Luther King Drive)

    b. = +310 feet   (the distance from the west side of Martin Luther King Drive to the east side of Sprague Avenue along First Street)

    c. = _____ feet   (the distance you found from the north side of First Street to the south side of Second Street along Sprague Avenue)

    d. = _____ feet   (the distance you found from the west side of Martin Luther King Drive to the east side of Sprague Avenue along Second Street)

    Answer: Add a, b, c, and d: 350 + 310 + _____ + _____ = _____ feet: the total outside perimeter of the shape made by the intersections of Martin Luther King Drive, First Street, Sprague Avenue, and Second Street.

Workplace Perimeters

Review Kim's work. First, he found the distances from the Loading Dock to the Laboratory. Then he found the distance from Storage II to the Employee Entrance and from Storage I to the Production Line.

Kim also found the <u>exterior dimensions</u> of his workplace and the meaning of the word *perimeter*. Then he found the perimeters of the building, the sidewalk, and the street boundaries.

To complete his plan, Kim must find the difference between the perimeter of Storage I and the perimeter of Storage II. Estimate the missing answers without using a calculator. Fill in the missing answers.

PROBLEM 3:

Find the outside dimensions of Storage I.

Step 1: Count the squares on the north side of Storage I _____ and multiply by 10 = _____ feet.

Step 2: Count the squares on the west side of Storage I _____ and multiply by 10 = _____ feet.

Step 3: Count the squares on the south side of Storage I _____ and multiply by 10 = _____ feet.

Step 4: Count the squares on the east side of Storage I _____ and multiply by 10 = _____ feet.

Step 5: The perimeter of Storage I is the total of all its outside dimensions.

   a. North side of Storage I = _____ feet

   b. West side of Storage I = _____ feet

   c. South side of Storage I = _____ feet

   d. East side of Storage I = _____ feet

   Answer: Total all sides of Storage I = _____ feet

PROBLEM 4:

Find all the outside dimensions of Storage II.

Step 1: Count the squares on the north side of Storage II _____ and multiply by 10 = _____ feet.

Step 2: Count the squares on the west side of Storage II _____ and multiply by 10 = _____ feet.

Step 3: Count the squares on the south side of Storage II _____ and multiply by 10 = _____ feet.

Step 4: Count the squares on the east side of Storage II _____ and multiply by 10 = _____ feet.

Step 5: The perimeter of Storage II is the total of all its outside dimensions.

    a. North side of Storage II = _____ feet

    b. West side of Storage II = _____ feet

    c. South side of Storage II = _____ feet

    d. East side of Storage II = _____ feet

       Answer: Total all sides of Storage II = _____ feet

PROBLEM 5:

Find the difference between the perimeter of Storage I and the perimeter of Storage II.

PROCEDURE:

Subtract the perimeter of Storage I from the perimeter of Storage II:

    _____ feet (Storage II perimeter)

  – _____ feet (Storage I perimeter)

  = _____ feet

Answer: The difference between the perimeter of Storage I and the perimeter of Storage II is _____ feet.

Rectangles: A Shortcut to Finding the Perimeter

Kim needs a faster way to find the perimeters of different shapes in his workplace. First he found dimensions and perimeters. Then he saw something about all the shapes on his place maps.

   * They all have four sides.

   * The sides opposite each other are always the same length. This kind of shape is called a <u>rectangle</u>.

EXAMPLE 2:

How can Kim cut his work in half and complete his plan on time?

Step 1: Kim understands that he does not have to know the dimensions of all four sides of a rectangle to find its perimeter. For example, he found that the dimensions of the north side of Storage II and the south side of Storage II were the same. Then he found that the dimensions of the west side of Storage II and the east side of Storage II were the same.

Step 2: All the shapes on Kim's map have two sides with the same dimensions. The north and south sides always have the same dimensions. The east and west sides always have the same dimensions.

Step 3: Since two dimensions are always the same, Kim finds that he only needs to measure two different sides of the shape to find the perimeter.

Step 4: Kim must only measure two sides instead of four. This means he can find perimeters in half the time. Finding two dimensions takes half the time of finding four dimensions.

EXAMPLE 3:

Kim wants to use this new way to find the perimeter of the Production Line. The perimeter of the Production Line equals the total of all its outside dimensions.

Step 1: The dimension of the north side of the Production Line = 70 feet.

Step 2: The dimension of the west side of the Production Line = 50 feet.

Step 3: The dimension of the south side of the Production Line is the same as the dimension of the north side of the Production Line = 70 feet.

Step 4: The dimension of the east side of the Production Line is the same as the dimension of the west side of the Production Line = 50 feet.

Step 5: Add the dimensions of all sides of the Production Line:

North side =   70 feet

West side   = +50 feet

South side = +70 feet

East side   = +50 feet

       Total: 240 feet

Answer: The perimeter of the Production Line is 240 feet.

PROBLEM 6:

Kim wants to use this new way to find the perimeter of Packaging. Estimate the missing answers without using a calculator. Fill in the missing answers.

Step 1: The north side of Packaging = _____ feet

Step 2: The west side of Packaging   = _____ feet

Step 3: The south side of Packaging = _____ feet

Step 4: The east side of Packaging   = _____ feet

Step 5: Add the dimensions of all sides of Packaging:

North side =   _____ feet

West side   = +_____ feet

South side = +_____ feet

East side   = +_____ feet

       Total: _____ feet (all sides of Packaging)

Answer: The perimeter of Packaging is _____ feet.

Chapter 6

The Shapes of the Workplace

In this unit, you will learn a quick way to find the perimeters of different shapes in Kim's workplace. You will also learn how to tell others about this shortcut.

In Kim's assignment, Kim was asked to make a plan to improve the Shipping and Receiving department. First he used an organizational chart—a people map—to help him find out how people worked together. Then he made a graph—a number map—to show others, in numbers, what he planned to do. Finally, he made a drawing—a place map—of his workplace to see how the work moved from place to place.

Workplace Rectangles

Kim has found that:

* All the shapes on his workplace map are rectangles.

* All these shapes have two or four equal sides.

* The two equal sides of these shapes are always opposite each other.

* He only needs to measure two of the four sides to find the perimeters of these shapes.

* The perimeter of each of these shapes equals the sum of all that shape's sides.

More Shortcuts to the Perimeter

In Kim's workplace, all shapes are <u>similar</u>. *Similar* means that the shapes are the same in general outline but do not have the same dimensions.

All the shapes in Kim's place maps are called rectangles. They have four sides, and the sides opposite each other are always the same length. The long side of a rectangle is the <u>length</u>, and the short side is the <u>width</u>.

All rectangles have four <u>right angles</u>. These angles are all 90 <u>degrees</u>. Many different types of shapes have four sides, but only rectangles have four right angles.

QUESTION:

If rectangles have four angles and all the angles have 90 degrees, how many total degrees do all the angles have in a rectangle?

Answer: _____ degrees.

EXAMPLE 1:

Find the the length and width of Employee Parking (see page 42).

Step 1: Length. Employee Parking is 27 squares long. Since the scale reads 1 square equals 10 feet, Employee Parking is 270 feet long.

> *Answer:* Length equals 270 feet.

Step 2: Width. Employee Parking is 4 squares wide. Since the scale reads 1 square equals 10 feet, Employee Parking is 40 feet wide.

> *Answer:* Width equals 40 feet.

PROBLEM 1:

Find the length and width of Manager/Administrator Offices. Estimate the missing answers without using a calculator. Fill in the missing answers.

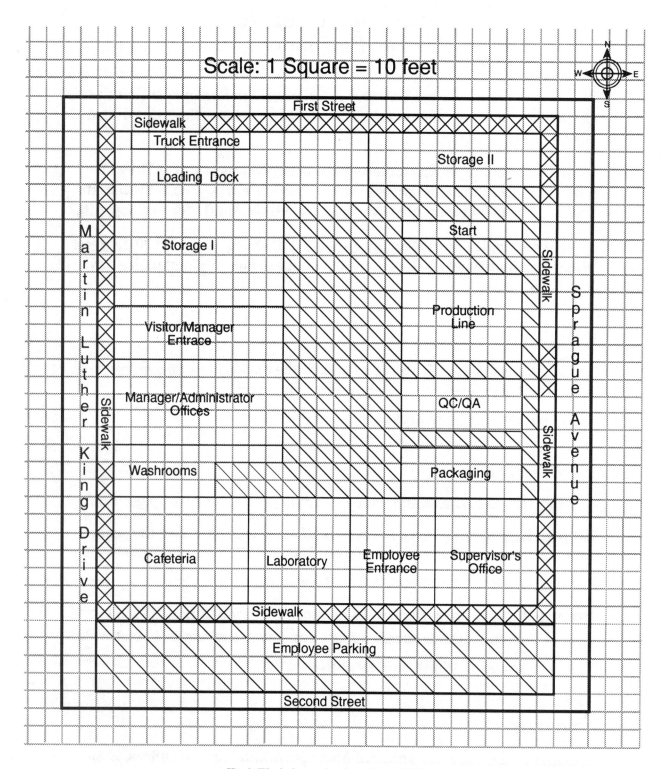

Scale: 1 Square = 10 feet

First Street

Sidewalk

Truck Entrance

Loading Dock

Storage II

Storage I

Start

Visitor/Manager Entrace

Production Line

Manager/Administrator Offices

QC/QA

Washrooms

Packaging

Cafeteria

Laboratory

Employee Entrance

Supervisor's Office

Sidewalk

Employee Parking

Second Street

Martin Luther King Drive

Sidewalk

Sprague Avenue

Sidewalk

Kim's Workplace—for Length and Width

Step 1: Length. Manager/Administrator Offices is _____ squares long, which equals _____ feet.

> *Answer:* The length of Manager/Administrator Offices equals _____ feet.

Step 2: Width. Manager/Administrator Offices is _____ squares wide, which equals _____ feet.

> *Answer:* The width of Manager/Administrator Offices equals _____ feet.

PROBLEM 2:

Find the length and width of the Cafeteria. Estimate the missing answers without using a calculator. Fill in the missing answers.

Step 1: Length = the number of squares _____ times 10.

> *Answer:* The length of the Cafeteria = _____ feet.

Step 2: Width = the number of squares _____ times 10.

> *Answer:* The width of the Cafeteria = _____ feet.

Showing Others How to Find Perimeters

Kim wants to teach Chirk and Lida how to find the perimeters of rectangles. He needs to find a way to find perimeters of rectangles that is simple, quick, and always the same.

EXAMPLE 2:

Kim wants to write simple instructions to help others find perimeters of rectangles. These instructions are written like a sentence. This kind of sentence is called a <u>formula</u>.

Kim's sentence for an easy way to find the perimeter of a rectangle: The perimeter of a rectangle equals two times its length plus two times its width.

Kim wants to shorten this sentence to make a formula.

Step 1: Kim drops words he does not need. He crosses words out of his original sentence:

> ~~The~~ perimeter ~~of a rectangle~~ equals two ~~times its~~ length plus two ~~times its~~ width.

This makes a new sentence:

> Perimeter equals two length plus two width.

Step 2: Then Kim makes abbreviations—like his initials—of some words left in the sentence. He shortens perimeter to *P*, length to *L*, and width to *W*.

Original: Perimeter equals two length plus two width.

New sentence: *P* equals two *L* plus two *W*.

Step 3: Kim then replaces the remaining words with math signs. He changes "equals" to =, "two" to 2, and "plus" to +.

From: *P* equals two *L* plus two *W*.

To: $P = 2L + 2W$.

QUESTIONS:

1. Do you think that this formula—$P = 2L + 2W$—will work on all rectangles?

2. Can you explain this formula to other people?

3. If Lida and Chirk use this formula, will they be able to find the perimeters of other shapes in the workplace?

Using Math Sentences

See how the formula $P = 2L + 2W$ works in the next three problems.

EXAMPLE 3:

Find the perimeter of Employee Parking.

Step 1: Kim found the dimensions of Employee Parking to be:

Length equals 270 feet.
Width equals 40 feet.

Step 2: Take Kim's formula of $P = 2L + 2W$ and replace L with 270 (the length in feet):

$$P = 2 \times 270 + 2W$$

Step 3: Take Kim's formula and replace W with 40 (the width in feet):

$$P = 2 \times 270 + 2 \times 40$$

Step 4: For $2L$, multiply 2×270.   Equals 540 feet.

Step 5: For $2W$, multiply 2×40.   Equals   80 feet.

Step 6: Add $2L$ (540 feet) + $2W$ (80 feet) to equal 620 feet.

Step 7: $P = 620$ feet.

Answer: The perimeter of Employee Parking equals 620 feet.

PROBLEM 3:

Find the perimeter of the Visitor/Manager Entrance.

Step 1: The dimensions are:

Length equals 100 feet.
Width equals 30 feet.

Step 2: Take Kim's formula and replace L with _____ (the length in feet):

$$P = 2 \times \text{_____} + 2W$$

Step 3: Take Kim's formula and replace W with _____ (the width in feet):

$$P = 2 \times \text{_____} + 2 \times \text{_____}$$

Step 4: For $2L$, multiply $2 \times$ _____ .   Equals _____ feet.

Step 5: For $2W$, multiply $2 \times$ _____ .   Equals _____ feet.

Step 6: Add $2L$ (_____ feet) + $2W$ (_____ feet) to equal _____ feet.

Step 7: $P =$ _____ feet.

Answer: The perimeter of the Visitor/Manager Entrance equals _____ feet.

PROBLEM 4:

Find the perimeter of the Employee Entrance.

Step 1: The dimensions are:

Length equals 50 feet.
Width equals 60 feet.

Step 2: Take Kim's formula and replace L with _____ (the length in feet):

$$P = 2 \times \text{_____} + 2W$$

Step 3: Take Kim's formula and replace W with _____ (the width in feet):

$$P = 2 \times \text{_____} + 2 \times \text{_____}$$

Step 4: For 2L, multiply 2 × _____ .   Equals _____ feet.

Step 5: For 2W, multiply 2 × _____ .   Equals _____ feet.

Step 6: Add 2L (_____ feet) + 2W (_____ feet) to equal _____ feet.

Step 7: $P =$ _____ feet.

Answer: The perimeter of the Employee Entrance equals _____ feet.

PROBLEM 5:

How much longer is the perimeter of the Employee Entrance than the perimeter of the Visitor/Manager Entrance? To find the difference, subtract the smaller perimeter from the larger.

Step 1: The perimeter of the Visitor/Manager Entrance = _____ feet.

Step 2: The perimeter of the Employee Entrance = _____ feet.

Step 3: Subtract the perimeter of the Employee Entrance from the perimeter of the Visitor/Manager Entrance.

Answer: The perimeter of the Visitor/Manager Entrance is _____ feet longer than the perimeter of the Employee Entrance.

Squares: A Special Type of Rectangle

All the shapes in Kim's workplace are rectangles. Although they may have different perimeters, they are all similar to each other.

Some of the rectangles have four equal sides. This kind of a rectangle is called a <u>square</u>. All squares are rectangles, but not all rectangles are squares.

Finding the perimeter of a square is similar to finding the perimeter of other rectangles.

EXAMPLE 4:

Kim wants to write simple instructions to help others find perimeters of squares. These instructions must be written like a sentence or a formula.

Kim's sentence for an easy way to find the perimeter of a square: The perimeter of a square equals four times the length of one of its sides.

Kim wants to shorten this sentence to make a formula.

Step 1: Kim drops words he does not need.

He goes from: ~~The~~ perimeter ~~of a square~~ equals four ~~times the~~ length ~~of one of its sides~~.

To his new sentence: Perimeter equals four length.

Step 2: Then Kim makes abbreviations of some words left in the sentence. He shortens "perimeter" to P and "length" to L.

From: Perimeter equals four length.

To: P equals four L.

Step 3: Kim then replaces the remaining words with math signs. He changes "equals" to =, and "four" to 4.

From: P equals four L.

To: $P = 4L$.

EXAMPLE 5:

Find the perimeter of the Laboratory.

Step 1: Kim found the dimensions of the Laboratory to be:

Length equals 60 feet.
Width equals 60 feet.

Step 2: Kim sees that the Laboratory is a rectangle. He also notices that all its sides are equal, which means that it is a square.

Step 3: Take Kim's formula for finding the perimeter of a square— $P = 4L$— and replace L with 60 (the length of one side in feet):

$$P = 4 \times 60$$

Step 4: For $4L$, multiply 4×60.   Equals 240 feet.

Step 5: $P = 240$ feet.

Answer: The perimeter of the Laboratory equals 240 feet.

QUESTIONS:

1. Do you think that the formula $P = 2L + 2W$ will work on squares?

2. Do you think that the formula $P = 4L$ will work on all rectangles?

3. Name the other square on the workplace drawing (Figure 14).

4. What is its perimeter in feet?

Math Practice II

In Kim's workplace we used dimensions to tell us length, width, and perimeters. Practice your skills with the following problems.

PROBLEM 6:

What is the length and the width of this rectangle? Scale: 1 square equals 100 feet.

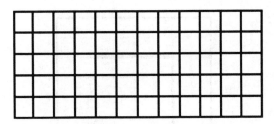

Answer: Length _____ feet. Width _____ feet.

PROBLEM 7:

Find the perimeter of this rectangle. Use the formula $P = 2L + 2W$. Scale: 1 square equals 1 foot.

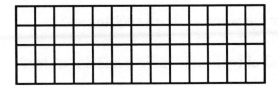

Answer: Perimeter _____ feet.

PROBLEM 8:

What is the perimeter of this rectangle? Use the formula $P = 2L + 2W$. Scale: 1 square equals 100 feet.

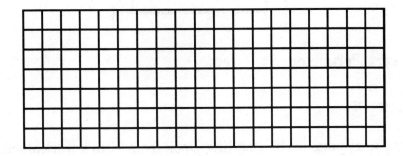

Answer: Perimeter _____ feet.

PROBLEM 9:

Find the perimeter of this rectangle. Use the formula $P = 4L$. Scale: 1 square equals 10 feet.

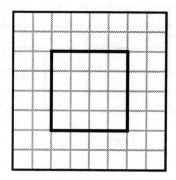

Answer: Perimeter _____ feet.

QUESTIONS:

1. Will this formula work with all rectangles?

2. Does this kind of rectangle have a special name?

PROBLEM 10:

This is the Truck Entrance to Kim's workplace. Find its perimeter. Use the formula $P = 2L + 2W$. Scale: 1 square equals 10 feet.

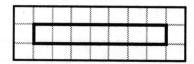

Answer: Perimeter _____ feet.

PROBLEM 11:

On the next page is the Loading Dock from Kim's workplace. This is not a rectangle, so you cannot use your formula for finding the perimeter. The scale is: 1 square equals 5 feet. Find the perimeter by adding up all the dimensions of all the sides.

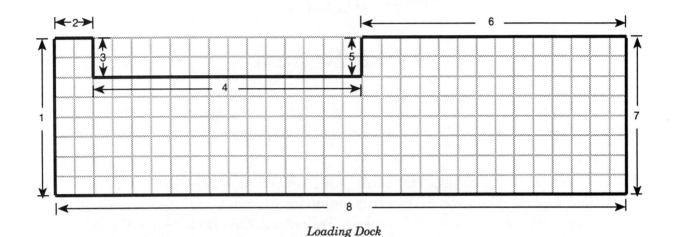

Loading Dock

Step 1: Find the dimensions of all the sides of the Loading Dock. Remember: Feet equals the number of squares times 5.

Side 1 = _____ feet   Side 5 = _____ feet

Side 2 = _____ feet   Side 6 = _____ feet

Side 3 = _____ feet   Side 7 = _____ feet

Side 4 = _____ feet   Side 8 = _____ feet

Step 2: Add up all the sides.

Answer: The perimeter of the Loading Dock = _____ feet.

Chapter 7

Final Report

Write the most important information from Kim's research in this final report. When you fill out this memo form, remember to look back at your work for the answers you need. Talk about the organizational chart, graphs, and drawing of the workplace.

Armond Tool Company Memo

Today's Date: _____

From [your name]: _____

Subject [from the overview]: _____

To: Janet, Shipping and Receiving Manager [you may include other people in the company as well]:

_____

_____

1. Overview. [Copy the Overview from Problem 4, Chapter 1.]

(continued)

---

2. People. [Suggestions for employee training. Offer ideas for changes in the organization.]

3. Numbers. [Explain in words what the graphs say in numbers.]

4. Places. [Give your ideas for changing the placement of the Loading Dock, Storage I, and Storage II.]

Chapter 8

A Case Study in Human Relations

Armond Tool is a good place to work. The company pays well, jobs are secure, the fringe benefits are good, and there is room for advancement.

But Kim has a problem because there do not seem to be clear lines of reporting. Sometimes he has trouble telling who's boss.

Janet, his boss and shipping and receiving manager, and Theodore, second shift manager, disagree. Kim is caught in the middle.

Janet says that the second shift quality control/quality assurance supervisor is not doing a good job because so many packages have been sent to the wrong customers. She thinks that to improve performance, the second shift quality control/quality assurance supervisor should work for Kim.

Theodore says that the second shift quality control/quality assurance supervisor is doing a good job and that shipping and receiving is the reason so many packages have been sent to the wrong customers. He thinks that the quality control/quality assurance supervisor should stay where he is.

What should Kim do?

Learning Diary

Now take some time to review your learning. Ask yourself about your learning plans and progress. What did you expect to learn when you began this book? What did you actually learn? What do you plan to learn next? There are no right or wrong answers.

Reading

READING OVERVIEW:

Reading is one of the most important skills you use in manufacturing. Answer these questions.

* Is reading now coming more easily to you?

* Have you enlarged your vocabulary?

* Can you find the meaning of words you do not know by using words you do know?

* Do you sound out difficult words?

* Are you better remembering what you read?

* Does your reading make sense?

* Do you understand special words used in the manufacturing workplace?

* Do you read on your own?

Your Reading Plans for the Future:

Name two specific steps you plan to take to improve your reading skills.

1.

2.

Writing

Writing Overview:

Reading and writing are both <u>communication skills</u>. Writing is often the best way to tell others what they need to know about the manufacturing workplace.

* Do you feel good putting your thoughts down on paper?

* Do you take notes on your reading?

* Is your writing making better sense?

* Can you write a good report on a manufacturing problem?

Writing Practice:

Write a two- or three-sentence paragraph about your job. Begin with a topic sentence and one or two facts that prove your point.

YOUR WRITING PLANS FOR THE FUTURE:

Name some ways you plan to keep on developing your writing skills.

1.

2.

Mathematics

MATH OVERVIEW:

In this unit, you worked with math that could be explained through different kinds of drawings.

* How much have you learned about working with numbers?

* Can you use math to prove a point?

* Can you read and draw a graph?

* Can you use your measurement skills to find dimensions on a map from a scale?

* Do you know how to substitute letters for numbers when finding the dimensions of rectangles and squares?

* Can you convert measurements from U.S. customary units to the metric system?

* Why should you be interested in working with the metric system?

* How far do you want to go in developing your math skills?

USING YOUR MATH SKILLS IN THE MANUFACTURING WORKPLACE:

* Can you make an estimate of approximate answers for problems in addition?

* Name two different kinds of graphs.

   1.

   2.

* If one square equals ten feet, how many feet do three squares equal?

   Answer: _____ feet

* Find the perimeter of a rectangle with a length of 16 feet and a width of 14. Use the formula $P = 2L + 2W$ to find your answer.

   Answer: The perimeter equals _____ feet.

* It is 13 miles from New York to Hewlett. What is this distance in kilometers? There are 1.6 miles in a kilometer.

   Answer: There are _____ kilometers between New York and Hewlett.

Reasoning

REASONING OVERVIEW:

   In this unit, you used reasoning skills to read scales and maps. From this information, you learned the relationships among people and among shapes and dimensions.

* Did you improve your skills in following directions?

* Can you see the relationship between graphs and numbers?

* Do you understand the relationship between scales and maps?

* How does an organizational chart show the relationships among people in the organization?

* Can you paint the big picture when you write a topic sentence overview for a report?

* Do you know how to use numbers to explain your big picture?

USING YOUR REASONING SKILLS:

Draw a chart that shows how work flows through a manufacturing workplace. Does the work flow make sense?

Your Future Learning Plans

In general, what do you plan to learn next?

What are your specific plans for:

1. Reading?

2. Writing?

3. Mathematics?

4. Reasoning?

Workplace Dictionary

Some of these words may be new to you. They were used in this book. They were underlined when they first appeared.

Each word is defined here in simple terms. Then it is used in a sentence.

These are "working definitions." Use your dictionary for more complete or <u>alternative</u> meanings for these words. You will find it very helpful to keep a notebook of other new words you come across in your reading.

Abbreviation: A short way of writing something. A common *abbreviation* for *book* is *bk*.

Alternative: Another way of doing or expressing something. There are often *alternative* ways to do the same job.

Bar graph: A graph that uses bars (stripes or bands) to picture the relationships among numbers. Kim used a *bar graph* to picture shipping figures.

Communication skills: The way we give information to others. The abilities to write and to speak clearly are important *communication skills*.

Computer numerical control: The application of computer technology to numerically controlled machine tools. A knowledge of computer machine technology is necessary to work with *computer numerical control*.

Convert: To change one thing to another. Sometimes it is necessary to *convert* meters to yards.

Data entry system: A way of getting information into a computer. Modern manufacturing workers must learn how to operate *data entry systems*.

Degree: A unit for measuring angles. A right angle has 90 *degrees*.

Dimensions: The length, width, and/or depth of an object. The *dimensions* of the rectangle were: length, 10 feet; width, 5 feet.

Exterior (or outside) dimensions: The dimensions on the outside of a shape. The *exterior, or outside, dimensions* of the workplace were 300 feet in length by 200 feet in width.

Flexible manufacturing: The application of a number of computer-based technologies in manufacturing. *Flexible manufacturing* requires a team effort and the ability to work with different kinds of machines.

Formula: A sentence written in math terms. Another word for *formula* is *equation.*

Global economy: The way business and manufacturing are tied together all over the world. Most manufacturing is done as part of the *global economy.*

Graph: A picture or map of numbers. *Graphs* are often used to illustrate a report. There are many different kinds of graphs, including bar graphs, line graphs, and pie charts.

Initials: A way of shortening words by just using the first letters. Some workers call Armond Tool by its *initials*—A.T.

Intersection: The place where things like roads or lines meet. During rush hour, the *intersection* of Sprague Avenue and Second Street is very busy.

Kilometer: A unit of length in the metric system. A *kilometer* equals about 1.6 miles.

Length: The distance from one end to another of something. In rectangles, the longer dimension. The *length* of the rectangle was 50 feet, while its width was 25 feet.

Line graph: A graph that uses a line to show the relationships among numbers. The *line graph* showed that the number of workers had dropped since 1990.

Loading dock: The area in a business building where trucks are loaded and unloaded. Two people are always on duty at the *loading dock.*

Manufacturing: Making or processing something with machinery. *Manufacturing* cars is a big business in the United States.

Master: To understand or control. All workers need to *master* basic math skills.

Meter: The basic unit of length in the metric system. One *meter* is about the same length as one yard.

Metric system: A system of measurement based on tens, used by most people outside the United States. Units such as centimeters, meters, kilometers, grams, and kilograms are used in the *metric system*.

On-line: Coming into use. A new data entry system is coming *on-line* at Armond Tool.

Organizational chart: A chart or map that shows how people in a group work with each other. Often an *organizational chart* shows things the way they should be, not the way they are.

Overview: A short and general statement that begins a report. A one-sentence *overview* can be made from a topic sentence.

Perimeter: The sum of all the outside dimensions of a shape. If the length of a rectangle is 10 meters and its width is 5 meters, the *perimeter* is 30 meters.

Personnel Department: The part of an organization that is usually responsible for employee benefits and other things that affect employees in a personal way. The personal records of the employees were kept in the *Personnel Department*.

Promote: To advance; to give a higher rank or importance to someone. Armond Tool *promoted* Kim to a more important job.

Quality Control/Quality Assurance: The persons or department responsible for making sure that a product is made the way it is supposed to be made. Successful manufacturers make a commitment to excellent *quality control/quality assurance* in making their product.

Rectangle: A four-sided shape whose opposite sides are the same size. All the angles in *rectangles* are 90 degrees.

Relationship: A connection between people or things. Graphs show the *relationships* of numbers; an organizational chart shows the *relationships* of people.

Right angle: An angle of 90 degrees. A square has four *right angles*.

Scale: A statement on a map or other drawing that explains the relationship between the dimensions on the drawing and the true dimensions of the object. Scales can also be called legends or keys. The *scale* on the map said that one inch on the map was equal to one mile in town.

Second shift: The group of workers whose hours begin later in the day and extend into the evening. Also, the time when these people work. The *second shift* works from 4 P.M. to midnight.

Similar: In the same basic shape but having larger or smaller dimensions. No matter how different in size, rectangles will always be *similar* in shape because they always have four 90-degree angles.

Square: A special kind of rectangle, with all four sides of the same length. Since all four sides were 3 feet long, the rectangle was a *square*.

Substitute: To replace one person or thing with another person or thing. In modern manufacturing, computers are often *substituted* for older ways of doing things.

Supervisor: A person who watches over and directs others. As *supervisor*, Kim directs the work done by Lida and Chirk.

Technology: Machines and ways of doing things that improve the speed and/or quality of work. The use of computers in manufacturing is an example of modern *technology*.

Width: The distance from one side to another of something. In rectangles, the shorter dimension. The length of the rectangle was 50 feet, while its *width* was 25 feet.

Work cells: A way of organizing machines. *Work cells* are used in high-tech manufacturing.

U.S. customary units: The way people in the United States usually measure, using units such as inches, feet, miles, ounces, and pounds. In many industries, *U.S. customary units* are being replaced by the metric system.

Work flow: The way work moves around the workplace. The real *work flow* and the way work is supposed to move are not always the same.

Appendix

Equivalents—U.S. customary units and metric units

Linear Measurements

1 centimeter = 0.3937 inches

1 meter = 39 inches

1 kilometer = 0.621 miles

1 inch = 2.54 centimeters

1 yard = 0.9144 meters

1 mile = 1.609 kilometers

Perimeters

To find the perimeter of a shape, add all its outside dimensions together.

Perimeter of a rectangle: $P = 2L + 2W$

Perimeter of a square: $P = 4L$

Answers

CHAPTER 1

Problem 1. **Step 2:**

a. accountant
b. administration
c. and
d. first
e. maintenance
f. manager/accountant
g. marketing
h. mechanic
i. second
j. shift
k. shipping/receiving
l. supervisor
m. vice president

Problem 2: The information you need to put the names on the chart is in the "Congratulations" section you were directed to in Step 1 of this problem.

Questions and Activities:

1. & 2. Use information from "Congratulations" to answer these questions.
3. Use your own ideas to answer this question.
4., 5., & 6. Use information from your own workplace for these activities.

Problem 3. **Step 3:** Use information from the sources mentioned in Steps 1 and 2 to answer Who, Where, and When about Kim's plan for improvement.

Problem 4: Your topic sentence, or overview, should include the answers to Who, What, Where, When, and Why about Kim's plan. Use the information you wrote in Problem 3.

CHAPTER 2

Questions: The section of Chapter 1 you are told to review will give you the answers to the questions.

Problem 1: 1995—9,000; 1996—11,000

Problem 2: Have your bars for 1995 and 1996 show the numbers you figured out for Problem 1.

Problem 3: 1993—100; 1995—180

Problem 4: Have your bars for 1993 and 1995 show the numbers you figured out for Problem 3.

Problem 5: Dot for 1995—at 9,000; dot for 1996—at 11,000. Connect dots with a line, in order of years, from 1993 through 1996.

Problem 6: Dot for 1993—at 100; dot for 1994—at 180; dot for 1995—at 180; dot for 1996—at 110. Connect dots with a line, in order of years, from 1993 through 1996.

Problem 7: Dot for 1990—at 12,000; dot for 1991—at 11,000; dot for 1992—at 9,000; dot for 1993—at 10,000; dot for 1994—at 9,000; dot for 1995—at 10,000. Connect dots with a line.

Problem 8: 1990—12,000; 1991—10,000; 1992—8,000; 1993—10,000; 1994—9,000; 1995—9,000

Problem 9: 1990—7,000; 1991—8,000; 1992—6,000; 1993—5,000; 1994—7,000; 1995—8,000

Problem 10: Dots at the figures given, connected with a line.

CHAPTER 3

Problem 1: Draw lines on Figure 11 as directed in Steps 1 through 5.

CHAPTER 4

Problem 1. **Step 1:** 280 feet **Step 2:** 280 [÷ 3 =] 93.3333 **Answer:** 93

Question: .3 or $\frac{1}{3}$

Problem 2: 10.4

Problem 3: 68.8

Problem 4: 35.635 **Answer:** 35.6 (rounded)

Problem 5. **Step 1:** 18 **Step 2:** 18 **Answer:** 180

Problem 6. **Step 1:** 7 **Step 2:** 7 x 10 **Answer:** 70

Problem 7. **Step 1:** 2 **Step 2:** 2 x 10 **Answer:** 20

Problem 8: a. 14 b. 2,100 c. 70

Problem 9:

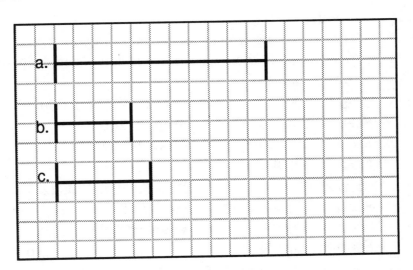

CHAPTER 5

Problem 1. **Step 1:** a. 27 b. 27 (x 10) **Answer:** 270
  Step 2: a. 29 b. 29 (x 10) **Answer:** 290
  Step 3: a. 27 b. 27 (x 10) **Answer:** 270
  Step 4: a. 29 b. 29 (x 10) **Answer:** 290
  Step 5: a. 270 b. 290 c. 270 d. 290

Problem 2. **Step 3:** 35; 350 feet **Step 4:** 31; 310 **Step 5:** c. 350 d. 310
  Answer: 350 + 310 + 350 + 310 = 1,320

Problem 3. **Step 1:** 10; 100 **Step 4:** 6; 60
  Step 2: 6; 60 **Step 5:** a. 100 b. 60 c. 100 d. 60
  Step 3: 10; 100 **Answer:** 320

Problem 4. **Step 1:** 10; 100 **Step 4:** 3; 30
  Step 2: 3; 30 **Step 5:** a. 100 b. 30 c. 100 d. 30
  Step 3: 10; 100 **Answer:** 260

Problem 5: 320 − 260 = 60

Problem 6. **Step 1:** 70 **Step 4:** 30
  Step 2: 30 **Step 5:** 70 + 30 + 70 + 30 = 200
  Step 3: 70 **Answer:** 200

CHAPTER 6

Question: 360 (degrees)

Problem 1. **Step 1:** 10; 100 **Answer:** 100 **Step 2:** 5;50 **Answer:** 50

Problem 2. **Step 1:** 8; 80   **Step 2:** 6; 60

Questions: 1. It will.

2. Try explaining it to other learners in your class.

3. Yes—because their workplace is composed exclusively of rectangles.

Problem 3. **Step 2:** 100   **Step 6:** 200; 60; 260

Step 3: 30; 100 (x) 30   **Step 7:** 260

Step 4: 100; 200   **Answer:** 260

Step 5: 30; 60

Problem 4. **Step 2:** 50   **Step 6:** 100; 120; 220

Step 3: 60; 50 (x) 60   **Step 7:** 220

Step 4: 50; 100   **Answer:** 220

Step 5: 60; 120

Problem 5. **Step 1:** 260   **Step 2:** 220   **Answer:** 40

Questions: You can answer these questions with information you have already read in this chapter.

Problem 6: Length 1,200 feet; width 500 feet

Problem 7: 34 feet

Problem 8: 5,200 feet

Problem 9: 1,600 feet

Problem 10: 160 feet

Problem 11. **Step 1:** Side 1 = 40   Side 4 = 70   Side 7 = 40

Side 2 = 10   Side 5 = 10   Side 8 = 150

Side 3 = 10   Side 6 = 70   **Answer:** 400

CHAPTER 7: FINAL REPORT

There are no right or wrong answers for this final report. Draw on the work you have done already to complete the report. Use the suggestions on each part of the report to help you.

CHAPTER 8: CASE STUDY

There are no right or wrong answers to this case study. Consider all possibilities.

LEARNING DIARY

Your answers to all questions in this section are completely your own, based on your own learning progress and plans.